To martha from
the Alcatraz School-
girl,

Anna Thumann

Alcatraz Schoolgirl

A Memoir
My Life on the Rock

Anna Thumann

ISBN: 1461087864
ISBN-13: 978-1461087861

DEDICATION

This book is lovingly dedicated to my family and friends who, in various ways, directly or indirectly, contributed to the contents of these memoirs.

CONTENTS

ACKNOWLEDGMENTS

My sincerest thanks to my best friend in the world, Walter Symons, who listened to my many reminiscences, read the stories after I put them into writing, and gave me the benefit of his expertise when changes needed to be made.

Also, I am grateful to my son, Ron, for his assistance and patience with his "technically challenged" mother when it came time to organize the material for printing; my granddaughter, Emily, for her ability to revive my mother's old Brownie Box Camera snapshots and make them usable in this book; my daughter-in-law, Meg, for her creative cover design.

Without the assistance and encouragement from these individuals, this book would not have been completed.

1 TAKE MY DAUGHTER.......PLEASE!

If ever there was a mother who had every right to want to give her kid away, it was my mother. In May 1934, my mother, sister, and I were scheduled to move out of the house we were renting in Odenton, Maryland. The train tickets were purchased, and we were anxious to move to California where my mother was going to marry my stepfather, and we would start a new life as a family on Alcatraz Island.

A couple of days before we were to leave, I woke up in the morning with my head throbbing. I was burning up with a high fever, and my mother was really concerned for me. At the same time she was at a loss as to what we should do about our move. She called the doctor to see if there was anything miraculous that could be done in order for us to travel. His diagnosis was that I was coming down with the measles and he would have to quarantine the entire family. A sign went up on the front door and we were stuck inside the house until I was well. That meant we had to delay our trip another ten days to two weeks.

The days went by, and according to the doctor's orders, the window shades had to be drawn and the room kept dark to protect my eyes until the fever subsided. A gloom hung over the entire household and I not only felt sick, but oh so guilty as well.

After about eight days I started to feel better, my sister hadn't come down with the measles yet, and it looked as though we were finally going to be off to California. We repacked our clothes, notified the landlord of the new date for our departure, and things were finally looking up for all of us. But, in the words of the old saying, "Don't count your chickens before they hatch," we soon found out there were still lots of chickens waiting to be hatched.

A day or two later my sister, Dorothy, and I hopped out of bed, got dressed, and ran downstairs to eat breakfast. My mother took one look at me and gasped, "what is the matter with your jaw?" She reached out with her hand and felt my face, and looked as if she were going to cry. "Anna, I am going to call the doctor again because I think you have the mumps." Sure enough, I had the mumps on one side, and we were all quarantined again for another ten days. The worst thing about it all was that my sister didn't catch the mumps, but ten days later I developed mumps on the other side of my face, and the quarantine was extended once again. Everyone had to be notified again to change our moving date, our travel date, and my mother's wedding date. And, just as a side note, while lying in bed and fooling around with my loose teeth, I was so startled when my two front teeth fell out, I swallowed them both. I was scared to death to tell my mother, so I just fretted, imagining that I was going to grow new teeth in my stomach. When I finally smiled and mother saw the vacancy in the front of my mouth, I confessed to her what had happened, and was relieved to find out that everything would "come out" all right.

After more than a month of quarantines and medical emergencies, we finally boarded the train for California. My soon-to-be stepfather met us at the train station in San Francisco, and we went directly to the Justice of the Peace where they were married. After taking us all out to an early dinner, we took a cab to the pier where we boarded the boat for the fifteen minute trip to our new home.

I can remember feeling like Shirley Temple embarking on a new and exciting movie adventure. There was no fear, no apprehension --- just happiness and excitement. I was only seven years old, and at that moment, life seemed really good.

2 MY FIRST INDIAN

The train pulled into the station with a loud swooshing sound, steam spewing from under the wheels, and then the screeching on the rails as it came to a stop at the Baltimore, Maryland station. My mother, sister and I were dressed in our travel clothes, holding our overnight bags containing toilet items we would need for the week ahead a tooth brush, tooth paste, soap, hair brush, and games to play when we got tired of looking out the window.

A friendly conductor, wearing a dark uniform with a red cap, helped us up the little stairs that led into the train, and then we were greeted by another man in a different uniform who showed us to our compartment in the Pullman car. Mother told us it was going to be a very long trip that would last five days and four nights before we would reach California. A whole new life lay ahead of us as a family living on Alcatraz Island.

The trip was uneventful as we settled into our daily routine on board the train. We washed up in the morning in our compartment, ate meals in the dining car, walked through the various railcars and talked with people, and played games. As darkness set in the porter would make up our bunks from the benches we had been sitting on most of the days, and then it was bedtime. I will always remember the comforting sound of the train wheels as they "clickety-clacked" over the rails. It was just like being rocked to sleep.

Crossing the Mississippi River, the train's wheels seemed as though they were going to sink right down into the water when the fully loaded train got on the tracks.   I was really afraid that we were going to sink to the bottom of the muddy, dirty looking river, and I didn't know how to swim yet.   But thank goodness we made it across without jumping the tracks, or tipping over, or drowning.

When we reached the other side of the river the scenery changed dramatically, and all we saw were miles and miles and miles of flat land full of corn and waving yellow grain, with absolutely nothing interesting to see.   My sister and I were really disappointed because in the western songs we sang in school, the plains were where the deer and the antelope played, and we didn't see any animals at all except for an occasional stray dog at a lonely country train station.   And where were the covered wagons, and giant buffalo we saw in all the movies? Oh well, it was back to the coloring books, crayons, and games.   We still had a long way to travel.

After three full days, we pulled into the station at Yuma, Arizona. It was extremely hot --- I think it must have been at least 300 degrees, because when we got off the train to walk around, the heat went right through the soles on my Mary Janes and actually felt as though it was going to burn my feet.   My mother and sister couldn't stand the intense heat and got back on the train.   Mother said that I could walk around for about ten minutes, but I should keep an eye on the window of our car so she could let me know when it was time to get back on board.   Jumping up and down just like I did at the beach when the sand was too hot for my bare feet, I found some shade under an awning near the entrance to the station and sat down on a bench to see how much money I had in my purse.   Maybe there would be enough to buy some candy or something in the store.   With my head bent down, while scrounging through the junk in the bottom of my purse, I noticed two very strange looking shoes appear on the ground right in front of me.   As I slowly raised my head to see what kind of person could be wearing such strange shoes, I looked straight into the heavily lined face of a very tall, very dark-tanned Indian man with a brightly colored blanket thrown across his shoulder.   I froze right there in my seat.   I was sure that I was going to be killed with a bow and arrows, scalped, and never see my family again.   After all, that's what I saw them do in the movies.   I guess the Indian saw the panic in my eyes

4

and very quietly said, "Hello little girl, what's your name?" I thought to myself that he didn't say "ugh" or "how" or anything like that --- he didn't even speak like a real Indian . With a shaky quiet voice, I said my name was Anna, and that I wasn't going to do anything wrong. I just wanted to buy something in the store and get back on the train because my mother was waiting for me and she'd get really mad if I was late. The Indian asked how much I planned to spend. I opened my hand and showed him the money clutched in my sweaty palm. He said I had just the exact amount to buy a real Indian papoose doll from him. I could hardly believe my luck. With papoose in hand I, in my Mary Janes, "hot- footed" it back across the sidewalk in front of the train station. I boarded the train and quickly found my mother and sister to tell them all about seeing a real live Indian and to show them my new Indian doll.

It looked as though living in the Wild West was going to be a real adventure alright, but somehow I now had the feeling that it wasn't going to be quite the same as it was in the Western movies I had seen.

3 A STITCH IN CRIME

In the spring of '34, when we were still in Maryland anticipating our trip to California, mother talked with us over a period of time and tried to prepare my sister and me for what was to come. In a short time we were going to be living in a new state 3,000 miles away from Maryland, in a new apartment, on an island in the middle of San Francisco Bay, with a new father, and a whole bunch of new rules to live by. My sister and I thought it was going to be tons of fun. After all, what do two little girls 7 and 5 years old care about as long as they are warm, well fed, and loved. But my mother was having all kinds of anxiety about everything. The task of setting up a new household under such unusual circumstances was going to involve a lot of adjustments on her part.

When we arrived daddy took us up to our living quarters and showed us all around. Then he sat Dorothy and me down and, in his usual easy manner, let us know from the very first day what the rules would be for my sister and me. We must absolutely never talk to any of the prisoners under any circumstances. We could play outside in areas near the family housing. We could not wear shorts or swimsuits anymore, or anything else that was skimpy in a suggestive way. And, all our laundry, except for "intimate" garments had to be sent to the prison laundry to be washed and pressed by the inmates. So mother bought one of those folding dryer racks from a store in San Francisco and put it in the bathroom where all our "girly" things could dry.

7

As time went by, my sister and I outgrew some of our dresses and mother tore them into large pieces to use as cleaning and dusting rags around the house. On one occasion, which my sister and I have never forgotten, mother tore up a dress and inadvertently sent the pieces, along with the regular weekly laundry, to the prison. When the laundry was returned, to our amazement, the pieces had been carefully sewn back together into a dress. We all laughed hysterically and went next door to show it to our neighbors. That's when we found out that the neighbors not only did not get their things repaired or sewn back together, but perfectly good clothes had been ripped, buttons removed, and sent back in unwearable condition. Apparently that was one of the many ways the prisoners took out their anger and frustrations against officers they did not like. It didn't take any of the families on the island long to understand all the little subtleties we encountered while living in this newly established maximum security federal penitentiary. After all, what could the guards do to punish the inmates --- lock them up??

My dad and I had many conversations about the infamous inmates incarcerated on Alcatraz. He explained to me that a number of the prisoners were not only smart, but because of pressures brought on by the great depression, they had channeled their intelligence into getting involved in various unlawful and lucrative activities.

As I look back on my years on the Island, I find it fascinating how so many clever and intelligent inmates could creatively find ways to circumvent the rules. Now I realize that these same things happen all around the world, and not just in my little world on Alcatraz.

Our second home, the cottage by the prisoner work area.

Our final residence was destroyed by a group of Native Americans
during their occupation of the Island in 1969-1971.

The first prisoners arrived in 1934. Building #64, where we first lived on the Island, overlooked the dock where the prisoners were being unloaded.

4 THE GANG'S ALL HERE

When were the guys daddy had been telling us about going to show up? Rumors were circulating for weeks that the first prisoners scheduled to come to the Island would arrive by train in August or September 1934. The Island personnel had been in the process of moving on and settling into their living quarters for several months, even though the government furnishings for the apartments had not arrived yet. For a week or so we slept on abandoned Army cots and mattresses, and used crates and boxes for our tables and chairs. The guards were issued uniforms, the prison was being staffed and supplied for the new occupants, and the excitement had been building for weeks. When the big day finally arrived, the women and children were ordered to remain indoors and out of sight, while the barge pulled alongside the dock and the prisoners disembarked. Even so, our curiosity was so great we were determined to find a way to sneak a peek at our new residents.

My family's apartment was on the second level of Building #64 at the very end of the balcony. The Dock Tower, which was one of the tallest, freestanding prison towers ever built, was right outside my bedroom window. My sister and I were five and seven years old at the time, and we excitedly huddled by the locked window overlooking the dock, our noses pressed against the glass to catch a glimpse of the prisoners. We watched the first trainload of occupants arrive. The railcars had been loaded on to a barge and then transported across the bay to the Island. Rumors ran wild that Al Capone was going to be among the first group to arrive, and everyone, including the kids, already knew a great deal about his notorious escapades. When the inmates were brought off the train and onto the dock we desperately tried to find him among the group but were unable to distinguish one from another. They were all dressed in the same prison garb, rather scroungy looking, with an unkempt growth of beard acquired during their four day trip from the Midwest. All the men were linked together by heavy leg irons with chains running between their legs to keep them in line. There was no way we could possibly recognize Al Capone from the rest, but we all tried to guess.

After the prisoners were transported to their refurbished Island home, counted in, and safely locked in their cells, we got the okay to leave our apartments. As foreign as all this was to the families who were now residents on the infamous Rock, life gradually settled into a routine that continued over the years until the prison was no longer considered necessary in 1963.

Contrary to what many people thought, there were many advantages to living on Alcatraz. The children were safely removed from busy streets and lived in a neighborhood where everyone knew everyone else. But, because of the close proximity to one another, we also knew everyone else's business. The view from our Island home was breathtaking and ever-changing. Over the years we watched the addition of the Golden Gate Bridge, San Francisco Bay Bridge, and the building of Treasure Island for the 1939 Exposition. As more families continued to arrive, the social hall became the gathering place for more and more activities. There were potluck dinners, and parties for Halloween, Christmas, and New Years. The guards got together to purchase a ping-pong table for the kids, and downstairs there were a couple of pool tables and a two lane bowling alley for the adults. As time went by, a very small canteen was established where we could buy things like candy, cigarettes, soda pop, and various other odds and ends. It was operated by the wives of some of the guards, who also manned the Post Office where we picked up our mail each afternoon. Even though the world was in the throes of a horrible depression, we had a warm and comfortable place to live, plenty to eat, good friends to play with, and so we children were completely oblivious to the negative aspects outside our protected world. We thought life couldn't get much better than that.

Sometime around 1990, I was watching a television program about Alcatraz Island, narrated by William Conrad. He was talking about the arrival of the first inmates to the Island and showed a picture of the barge pulling into the dock. There in the window by the Dock Tower were two little girls huddled together taking in everything that was going on below them. I was so surprised to see that someone had captured a glimpse of my sister and me, and nearly sixty years later, there we were on TV.

As my life evolves, it seems as though time has been caught up in the strong currents that continually flow through the Golden Gate. Those long gone years may have been washed away with the outgoing tides, but the memories of an unusual and happy childhood remain as new and fresh as ever.

5 ROUND THE WORLD CHARLIE

There wasn't a school on the Island, consequently the children would have to cross the bay on a boat each day to attend school in San Francisco. This posed a problem for the families on Alcatraz who were still unfamiliar with both the city and the school system. Where and how to get the children there was a big problem, since some of them were just starting grammar school. How could reliable transportation be arranged for kids who were only five, six and seven years old, when school was so far away from home? Obviously parents couldn't leave the island every day and take them to school, and then wait in the city until three o'clock in the afternoon to take them home.

After much deliberation, it was discovered that one of the guards had spent time in San Francisco and was acquainted with a friendly cab driver. He volunteered to contact him to see if something could be arranged to transport the children. When the cabbie showed an interest in the job, he met with the parents, made a pick-up and delivery schedule, and negotiated his weekly pay. Then the names of the kids, along with all the required vital information, were provided to the school. Also, each teacher was given the responsibility for getting her student in the cab immediately after school.

The first week parents took turns going over with the kids on the 7:30 a.m. launch, introducing them to Charlie, the cab driver, reminding them about the rules for behavior in the cab, and instructing

15

the driver to wait with the kids on the dock until they had all boarded the launch for the return trip.

It took a few weeks for the parents to feel comfortable with the situation, but as time went by the routine became a way of life. I seem to remember that there were about five or six of us who went to Grant School, which was quite a distance from the dock, and Charlie was very reliable, friendly, funny, and enjoyed his Alcatraz kids.

As the school year progressed, there were days when the school schedule varied because of teacher conferences, or minimum days. Charlie took it all in stride, and thought of lots of ways to keep his charges from getting bored or rowdy. There were many exciting things going on in the city during the early 30's, and he would take us on "surprise adventures" to kill the time until the boat arrived.

We drove through the Presidio to watch the construction of the Golden Gate Bridge, and he would tell us stories about when it would open, how we would be able to walk across to Marin County, or drive across if our parents had a car. Only a few parents had cars since the guards worked six days a week and it wasn't practical to have a car for use just a few days a month, as well as pay rent for a garage near the dock in the city.

We went to the piers to see the gigantic cruise ships that were in port, and watch the passengers boarding for Los Angeles, Mexico, or maybe even the Hawaiian Islands. Since it was in the afternoon, we went further down the waterfront to visit the fishing boats as they were arriving back from sea to unload their catch-of-the-day. And, when there was a lot of time to kill, we drove out to see Fleishhacker Pool, Sutro Baths, and Playland at the Beach. Charlie even gave each of us a nickel to spend on candy if we had a good report card.

On shorter trips from school, Charlie taught us how to sing songs like "Row, Row, Row Your Boat" in two part harmony. The back seat sang and then was followed by the front seat. Another thing he taught us was an old saying we learned to chant about the last day of school. "No more pencils, no more books, no more teachers' dirty looks." I remember my mother wasn't too pleased with that one, but the kids loved it – we felt kind of naughty when we sang it.

Because of the wonderful times we spent each day throughout the school year with Charlie, we very quickly nicknamed him "Round the World Charlie." I don't remember if he was young or old, tall or short, fat or thin, but I do remember him as one of the nicest, friendliest people who took very good care of his precious cargo for approximately three years. We never envied any of those poor city kids who had to take the school bus or walk to school. Round the World Charlie, with his friendly greeting and enthusiasm, always made going to school a daily adventure for his Alcatraz kids.

6 OVER THE WAVES TO SCHOOL

It was 7:15 a.m. and I knew if I didn't hurry I'd miss the boat. With my warm jacket on, my bandana protecting my hair from the wind, and my binder and books securely held on my hip, I flew down the long flight of stairs to the dock. The other kids on the Island were already loading on to the launch for the fifteen minute trip to San Francisco. I learned very young in life to always be on time, because ten seconds late meant you literally missed the boat. Our boat was a 65 ft. launch named The McDowell. It had two main cabins. The front cabin was usually filled with parents and guards on their way to enjoy a day in the city, but the school bound kids chose to climb down the hatch into the back cabin. Benches lined both sides of the small cabin, with several windows directly above them. During the spring and fall the bay was usually pretty calm at that time of the morning, unless there were larger boats or ships on the bay and we had to cross their wake. Then the launch would roll and bounce around, with water sloshing over the windows giving the illusion we were on a sinking ship. After the first few months of taking the trip, we got over our apprehensions, grew accustomed to the many moods of the bay waters, and learned to have a lot of fun with it. We yelled and screamed as we bounced around, and the older boys often favored us with naughty, raunchy sea shanties that we never ever mentioned to our parents. I can only recall three days over a ten year period of time when the water was so choppy that the launch couldn't get close enough to the ramp for us to safely board. The prison office had to notify the schools of our absence, and we were free as the birds just to play all day.

I remember one time in particular, about five minutes into the trip, one of the boys took a mouse out of his jacket pocket and let it loose in the cabin. All of us girls shrieked as we jumped on the benches, and all heck broke loose as the boys chased the mouse around the cabin. The guard, who was sitting on the back deck, came "flying" down the hatch to investigate and wasn't the least bit amused by what he saw. All ten of us got a lecture about proper behavior on the boat. Needless to say, the boy who brought the mouse on board paid dearly for his escapade.

All in all, the kids always enjoyed the ride across the bay, but most of the mothers did not. My mother, for instances, was deathly afraid of the water, didn't know how to swim, and often got very nauseous on her many trips to the City. She much preferred the larger boat, The General Frank M. Coxe, nicknamed by the kids, The Coxie. I don't remember its length, or whether it was a boat or a ship, but it belonged to the Army. It had two very large cabins. The back cabin had really nice leather seating areas, and was restricted to Army officers from Ft. Mason and Angel Island, and the top ranking officials from Alcatraz Island. All the rest of us "common folks" rode in the front cabin with its wooden benches and battleship linoleum floors. The hold of the Coxie carried all the supplies needed for the Islands, as well as purchases made by the residents while in the city.

Periodically the Coxie and the McDowell had to go to dry dock to have the barnacles scraped from their hulls, and we rode replacements while the work was being done. I still remember the names of all those boats. There were two water barges, The El Aquario and The El Aguador. They were large flat looking barges that carried water to the Island to replenish our water supply. There was no fresh water available other than the water stored in a gigantic water tank on top of a hill on the north side of the Island. The kids loved riding the water barges because they created very large wakes. During the springtime the porpoises frolicked and played alongside the barges all the way across the bay. If it wasn't too rough, we were allowed to stand on the deck and watch them lead us all the way to the Island.

A tugboat named The Slocomb was also a frequent substitute. It was the slowest of all the boats we rode to school so we nicknamed it "slow come, slow go." When I was about nine or ten years old I had to get my first pair of glasses. They didn't have any correction to my vision, but my mother said they were to correct and strengthen the muscles in my eyes. When the glasses were fairly new, I dropped them on the floor of the cabin when I was rushing to get off, and didn't discover the loss until I got to school. When I went to the dock after school to go home, I was shocked to see the Coxie was back in service. I knew my mother was going to "have a fit" when I got home, so with tears streaming down my face I asked the captain of the Coxie how I could get my glasses off The Slocomb. He told me that the tug had left a few hours earlier to guide a ship back to Alaska, and it would not return for several months. Well, I was right about my mother, and I had to go without any glasses while we waited for the return of The Slocomb. About four or five months later The Slocomb showed up to take us to school and the Captain found me and returned my glasses. Boy was I relieved. Then I knew why it was so important to my mother to put my name inside absolutely everything I owned, wore, or carried with me.

I remember thinking as a child how much fun it would be to ride in automobiles and streetcars to school every day like all the other kids. As I look back on those days, I have such wonderful memories of riding the waters across San Francisco Bay on my many trips to the City. Now I realize I was the one who had all the fun.

The boat schedule for the McDowell and the General Frank M. Coxe.

The 65 foot launch, the McDowell was renamed Warden Johnson.
(Photo Don Bowden)

The tugboat the Slocomb

The General Frank M. Coxe

7 SEASONS OF MY YOUTH

Oh, how we loved the changing seasons! Just about the time we started to get a little bored with what we had been doing for a couple of months, the season changed and we enthusiastically plunged into different types of activities to consume our playtime on the Island. We had such rich and fun filled lives. We didn't have to go to the city to buy things to play with …. we had the satisfaction and joy of making our own from whatever we could find. Even though we were a small group of kids, and a wide range of ages, we came up with inventive and exciting things to do that involved all of us, throughout the seasons of the year.

In the FALL we played flag football, kick the can, jump rope (especially double Dutch). And, of course, we were busy getting back into the routine of riding the launch back and forth to school in San Francisco.

Because of the windy, blustery, cold weather we experienced on the Island during the WINTER, most of our activities were indoors. We gathered at one another's homes and played monopoly, card games, built model planes, and listened to all the scary radio programs like "Lights Out" and "Inner Sanctum."

SPRING was fantastic for flying kites and riding down the hills on our coasters, which we made from orange crates discarded from the

Island's canteen, wheels rescued from old roller skates and broken doll carriages.

SUMMER was definitely the season for roller skating and all the games we could invent to play on skates. It was the greatest time of all. We all had ball bearing skates, a can of oil, and a skate key which hung from our neck on a string. During the summer the weather on and around the Island was very cold, foggy, and windy. The wind gusting through the Golden Gate and across the Island was wonderfully strong. Each day that the conditions were right, we would gather on the old army parade ground, where the cement was flat and smooth from many years of use, and we would pair up for an afternoon of the greatest thrills a group of kids could experience.

After putting on our skates, squeezing fresh oil from the cans into the little holes in the wheels, tightening the clamps onto the soles of our shoes with our keys, we were ready to go. Oh yes, and the most important piece of equipment for our game was either an old bed sheet or one of the many blankets left behind in the living quarters by the army when they moved from the Island. With everything in readiness, we would skate over to the west side of the parade ground, each pair of kids would grab a side of their blanket, hold it up in the air to catch the wind like the spinnaker on a sailing ship, and fly like the dickens across the entire distance of the parade ground until we slammed into the sea wall on the far side of the Island. We felt a sense of freedom, excitement, and exhilaration that was unmatched. We laughed, and hugged, and celebrated our safe flight, then put up our sails to fly over and over again until the sun was setting below the Gate and our mothers called us home for dinner.

Each season was a time we relished and enjoyed to the fullest. We were families thrown together by chance on a very small and isolated island. We shared each others sorrows and happiness, and through the closeness of our existence, we became an extended family in every sense of the word. We shared a bond that is difficult to explain today in light of the modern lifestyles.

For over seventy-five years we still keep in touch with one another through an Alcatraz Alumni Newsletter, and each July the "kids" from the Island have a reunion. We all laugh at the looks on the faces of passersby as they read the sign that states, "PICNIC SITE – ALCATRAZ ISLAND REUNION." Needless to say, they cut a wide path around our area, leaving us to enjoy our "family."

Playground equipment made by the prisoners.

8 CHRISTMAS ON THE ROCK

On the one hand I wanted desperately to believe there really was a Santa Claus, but I also wanted to feel that I was smart enough to be in on the secret. I was nine years old and I didn't want to look like a little "Dumb Dora" if Santa only existed in fairy tales. I thought about it a lot that year and as Christmas approached I decided that the safest thing to do was to go through the motions as though I believed, but deep down inside, and in conversations with my girlfriends, I was much too old to fall for that story. That way I had all the bases covered...just in case.

Christmas shopping in the city was always a ritual I enjoyed very much. My sister, Dorothy, and I would save our allowance, plus money we earned watching the younger children on the playground, while our mothers sat gossiping, doing their nails, darning socks, or whatever older ladies did when they were gathered in a group on the stairs. When the big day came, my mother, sister, and I went to San Francisco to Woolworths and Kress' dime stores for the big purchases. Dorothy and I each had a list of everyone we had to buy presents for....Mother, Daddy, Sister, and grandparents.

My mother would wait in front of the store while Dorothy and I split up and went our separate ways so we could not see what the other was buying. When we finished our lists, we met mother at the door and then went back inside Woolworths to have something to eat at the lunch counter.

On our way to catch the streetcar for the ride back to the dock, we would stop at the Crystal Palace Market for our Christmas tree. When we found the perfect tree, mother paid for it and asked to have it delivered to the dock for shipment to Alcatraz Island. The clerk was temporarily at a loss for words, but then with a look of disbelief would say, "yeah, that's very funny, now what's your real address?" My mother had to show him her prison I.D card before the clerk was convinced we really lived there.

Mother and Daddy did their shopping on a day when they went to the city by themselves. Their purchases were delivered to the dock on a weekday when all the kids were in school. Well, that's the way it was supposed to happen. A few weeks before Christmas I sent my letter to the North Pole requesting a gray wicker baby buggy I had seen in the Sears Christmas Catalogue. I fell in love with it and wanted it so badly that I could taste it. Again, to cover all the bases, I asked Santa for it, I prayed for it in Sunday school, I secretly mentioned it every single night in my bedtime prayers, and for the time being, I was dedicated to being an exceptionally good girl. I wasn't going to take any chances.

On the last day of school, before the start of the Christmas holidays, a group of us girls walked down to the dock to take the 4:30 p.m. boat home. We usually took the 3:30 p.m. launch, but because we stayed at school a little longer that day to help with the classroom party, we rode home on the General Frank M. Coxe, a much larger boat that went from Ft. Mason, to Alcatraz, and then to Fort McDowell on Angel Island. As we climbed the gangplank to get on board, a large delivery truck was loading merchandise in to the hold of the boat and there was a gray, wicker baby buggy, just like the one I had asked Santa to bring me for Christmas. I was very upset at what I saw, but decided it would be best not to say anything to my parents because I didn't want to do anything that might "mess up" the holiday.

Christmas Eve was the most festive time on the Island. All of the kids practiced singing carols at Iva Mckean's house for weeks, and now we were ready for our big night. We all gathered on the top balcony of Building #64 overlooking the dock and serenaded the 7:00 p.m. "Coxie" as it pulled in to the dock to pick up passengers going to the city. The captain held up the departure so that we could sing several carols, then everyone on the boat yelled and applauded as the boat tooted its horn and pulled away from the dock. We then followed Mrs. Mckean and serenaded all of the homes on the island. Towards the end of the route, we sang for the chaplain's family, the doctor's family, and finally for the warden and his family. Their house sat on the very top of the hill, beside the prison and opposite the lighthouse. They had a very large glass enclosed porch and it always held the tallest Christmas tree I had ever seen, gleaming with hundreds of colored lights and nearly filling the porch in all its glory. The warden and his family would have us circle the tree, hold hands, and sing several of their favorite carols. Then the prisoners, who worked in his house as trustees, would come out of the kitchen bearing several large trays of cookies and candies they made just for the occasion, and passed them around to all of us. As we filed out the door, we sang our way down the hills to the social hall for a party, which the guards and their wives put on for the kids. We had lots of food, games, and singing, and finally the high point of the night was the arrival of Santa Claus. Of course, all of us older kids knew that Santa was really Mr. Schnieder, the lighthouse keeper, but we couldn't care less as long as he had a present for each one of us in his bag.

As the hour grew late, it was time for everyone to go home to get a good night's sleep. Soon the children were snuggled down in their warm beds dreaming of all the goodies that Santa would bring them, and the parents began assembling wagons, and scooters, and quietly putting the presents under the trees. In our house, the first one awake in the morning had to awaken everyone else, and we went to the living room together. I can still remember the mixed feelings I had when I saw that gray wicker baby buggy sitting beside the tree. I was so happy to finally get it, but so sorry that my hunches were right and there really wasn't a Santa Claus. I felt as though something magical had been taken from my life. But the more I thought about it, the more grown up I began to feel. After all, anyone with any sense would know that Santa can't fly around the sky with a sleigh and eight reindeer, anymore than the Easter Bunny can lay chicken eggs and deliver jelly beans and chocolate candy. I didn't know if growing up was going to be as much fun as I thought it would be. But then I reminded myself that someday I would finally be old enough to wear silk stockings, Tangee lipstick, and fit in a brassiere, and I decided that growing older might possibly have some redeeming qualities after all.

31

Sunday School Christmas pageant. My sister, Dorothy
is on the bottom right. I am standing above her.

A group of younger kids at Halloween. Dorothy is in
the back row, third from the left.

Easter on the Island.

9 SHARING A ROOM WITH MY SISTER

I always wanted to sell my sister to anyone who was willing to buy her. I would have even traded her for a brother if that were the only deal I could make.

My sister could make me so angry. I thought she was the messiest, noisiest, tattletale anyone could be stuck with. She was only two years younger than I, but it might as well have been twenty. I was eleven years old, and thought I should not have to put up with all her nonsense.

One night we were having an argument in our shared bedroom, and I told her that I had put up with her mess long enough. I never, ever wanted to see her junk on my side of the room again. I took our jump rope out of the closet and tied it to the exact middle of the vanity table, pulled it across the room and tied it to the knob on the closet door, and then draped a sheet across the rope. The line had been drawn in the proverbial sand, and I dared her to cross it. The only problem was that her side of the room was where we entered, and I had to walk through her mess and crawl under the rope before I could get to my neat and tidy side. It did take care of our problem until we needed the rope to go play jump rope.

By that time, though, she had gotten the point and whenever she got out of line I didn't have to say a word. I just kicked her stuff back over the invisible rope, and the problem was solved.

All five pictures are of Dorothy my YOUNGER sister and me. Our mother insisted on dressing us alike as often as possible. And I HATED it. After all, I was two years her senior!

Top left: Dorothy and me with a guard. Top right: here we are with my mother. Bottom: some of the new kids on the Island sitting on the seawall in the mid '30s.

10 LET'S PRETEND!

"Come on, Betty, let's go outside and find something else to do. I'm tired of playing Chinese Checkers."

"Okay, but it's freezing. Let me get my jacket first. Do you want an apple? My mother got a whole crate of apples in the city yesterday."

"No, thanks, but will you hurry up! You're always lolly-gagging around. Betty, has your dad said who's going to move into the doctor's house? They've been gone quite a while and nobody's moved in yet."

"I don't know, but the other day when I was outside I found a window that was left unlocked at their house. I didn't go inside, but I nearly did. Let's go take a look and I'll show you the window."

We were two well-behaved ten-year-old girls, growing tired of the summer vacation from school, looking for something different to occupy our time until we had to go home for dinner. We walked out of Betty's house and slowly sauntered up the hill, taking the road that ran parallel with the prison, and stopped at the first house on our left. On the top of the hill was the lighthouse. Opposite it was the warden's house, then a short distance down the hill was the chaplain's house, and below it the doctor's residence.

Betty led me around the side of the house, past the bushes, and sure enough there was a window unlocked that led into the downstairs living quarters of the house. Giggling and nudging each other on, we climbed through the window and walked through the kitchen, living room, dining room and entrance hall.

"Wow," we both exclaimed at the same time. The house was still completely furnished - just like it was when the family lived there. The doctor's house was a lot bigger than ours. It had a full sized dining room with a glittering chandelier, and lots of chairs around the large table. I remembered seeing a room like that in one of those high society movies.

I nudged Betty towards the buffet and said, "I wonder if there is anything in the drawers." We quickly opened the top drawer and to our amazement we found all the linens for the big table. The next couple of drawers and cabinets held the dishes, glasses, candles, and silverware. Totally elated, we felt as though we had found a king's treasure.

I took a beautiful lace tablecloth out of the drawer and spread it over the table while Betty excitedly placed the dishes, silverware, and glasses into place. When we finished it looked so elegant – just like we were expecting "hoity-toity" guests for a fancy dinner party. Betty said, "Anna, the only thing missing are the flowers. You go outside and pick some from those bushes, and I'll find a vase to put them in."

As I climbed out the window a big hand reached over and grabbed my arm. "What do you think you are doing in this house, Anna? Come with me to the prison office where I can call your dad." Just then Betty yelled from the dining room, "What's taking you so long? Hurry up!" The guard recognized the other voice and took me, speechless and shaking, back inside the house. Betty was so startled to see us that she looked like a deer caught in the headlights.

Mr. Rose, with a very stern look on his face, but smiling on the inside, I'm sure, said, "Well, the two of you haven't done any damage, but you'll have to put everything back where you found it and then I will take you home to your parents."

We felt mortified, embarrassed, and scared, and after a lengthy lecture reminding us about right from wrong, we promised them that we had learned our lesson and wouldn't do anything like that again.

We were both confined to our homes for a week, and when we finally got "sprung," we got back to our Chinese Checkers, and jacks and jump ropes with all the energy and glee of two repentant and reformed ten year old girls.

11 THAT HAUNTING CLANK IN THE CLINK

Oh how I looked forward to all the holidays. Not for the reasons you might imagine, but because on holidays we got to go see the movies in the prison. The only theater on the Island was the chapel in the prison where the inmates attended church services for the various denominations. But on holidays, the prisoners were able to attend a movie in the afternoon and then the Island personnel could attend in the evening.

We all knew in advance which movie would be playing that evening. Our families had to plan for an early dinner, what snack to take, and all of us kids would decide with whom we would sit at the show. I can remember when I was in my pre-teens wishing and hoping and dreaming about which one of the Island "hunks" would accidentally sit next to me. All the girls at one time or another had crushes on all the boys who lived there, but no big romances, and no marriages ever resulted while I was living there. Since the Island was so small, and the families were so close, we really felt more like brothers and sisters in a large extended family.

The movie was scheduled to begin at 6:30 p.m. for the Island personnel, so there was usually about 30 or 35 adults and children gathered outside the main gate to the prison well before the designated time. Precisely at 6:30 p.m. the guards would usher us into the main office, count each and every one of us, and then move us into a holding cell. Then we heard that awful, dreaded, resounding clank of the cell doors closing behind us. We were counted again, moved into the next holding cell, and then that clank one more time. The next move was into the Chapel, where we quickly took our seats on the benches, and got ready for an evening of fun. Obviously, the movies were carefully selected because they never showed any violence, or weapons, or anything like that to the prisoners. So, we saw every Shirley Temple movie ever made, and movies like Test Pilot with Spencer Tracy, who put his gum on the side of the plane for good luck, and wore a long flowing white scarf around his neck. And then there were all those wonderful Fred Astaire and Ginger Rogers musicals. As an added attraction, if we were lucky, we would see an adventure film made by Father Bernard Hubbard about his expeditions in the Alaska Wilderness.

I always enjoyed all of the movies, but really got hooked on Father Hubbard's movies. He was a frequent visitor to the prison chapel, and his adventures became very personal for all of us. Father Hubbard was a Jesuit priest who flew to a remote Alaska crater to study and map its interior. I vividly remember one of his movies about a time when his plane was dangerously short on fuel, so in desperation the pilot took off and headed straight for the plume of steam, riding the thermal well clear of the crater. They floated down next to a fishing boat and borrowed enough fuel to continue on. Frequently the crater erupted sending plumes of ash into the air. Father Hubbard continued to return to the area he loved so well, and described it as being like a prelude to Hell. I remember telling my mother and dad that particular comment, but I got Holy Heck for saying the word He_ _. It was Ok for Father Hubbard to say it, but apparently not OK for me.

When the movie was finished, we were escorted back outside the gates through the same process we entered. As I look back on those holiday trips to the prison, I realize I learned a few valuable lessons that have remained deep in the recessed corners of my mind. First of all, I shall never forget the sound of the closing of those prison cell gates. There was such a finality to the sound. At least we knew we were going to be able to leave after a couple of hours. The other lessons learned were if you didn't show up on time, you would be left behind. And, be sure to go to the bathroom before you went to the movie. If you had to be escorted out anytime during the show, you were not allowed back in. To this day, I have a reputation of always being on time, and my bladder is trained to restrain any urges during any performance, waiting urgently for the intermission or "The End."

Over the years, it is amazing the lessons we learned, where and how we learned them, and the lasting impressions they made on our everyday existence.

12 A STAR IN "CHINATOWN"!

The spotlight shone on the Helene Hughes dancers. Their gorgeous makeup, glamorous costumes, and dancing feet wove a spell over the entire audience. They transported my mind to a different world and they mesmerized me. My small body was sitting quietly in a seat at the Golden Gate Theater, but inside I was dancing every step along with them, and I knew that when I got home I would imitate everything they did on stage to perfection.

The Golden Gate and Warfield theaters were two of my favorite places to go in San Francisco. Even at the young age of nine I was so impressed with the live theater, and the exposure films provided me to a variety of locations, cultures, and talents that were so foreign to my every day life. My girlfriend, Betty, and I shared information about every movie and vaudeville show we saw, and then we would spend hours rehearsing with one another in preparation for a time when we might be able to "put on a show" for our friends.

On the Island there was a place we called Chinatown. The kids gave it that name because it was located in the bowels of Building #64 and was covered by a heavy iron grating. Building #64 was the original barracks that was located directly above the dock area. When the Island was converted from an Army facility to a Federal Penitentiary in '34, the building was used to house the new guards and their families. There were three stories of living quarters, and then the bottom floor was deep underground, very dark and foreboding. As children we thought that if we had been able to get below the grating and start digging we would end up on the other side of the world in China, hence the name Chinatown.

On the stairway leading about halfway down to Chinatown there was a large opening in the stone wall about the size of a small window. At the bottom of the stairway was an entrance, which led into one of the small dungeons, scattered throughout the bottom of the building. Betty and I would prepare to practice our performances by dressing up in anything we could find that looked glamorous --- a ribbon for our hair from the top of a candy box, lipstick for our lips and cheeks, my dad's fedora would serve as a top hat, and a twig from a tree for a walking stick. Then we would take turns. Betty would sit outside the dungeon on the stairs and shine a flashlight through the hole in the wall as a spotlight on me while I performed my song or dance routine. The dungeon was just like an echo chamber and my voice sounded full and joyous, and my tapping feet flew across the cement floor in perfect rhythm to the imaginary music. And, for those moments, I was in my glory.

Then Betty and I would switch places and it would be her turn to be the star, and my turn to man the spotlight. We always knew the words to all the newest songs, because Betty's mom would buy a song sheet for us from one of the vendors on Market Street in San Francisco. The song sheet didn't have the music, but it had all the words to the latest "hit parade" songs from the radio, and songs from the most recent movie musicals.

The hours we spent in our magical world were unbelievably exhilarating. As we sang and danced to our imaginary theater orchestra, and bowed to the applause of our enthusiastic audience, our faces glowed with a sense of fulfillment that radiated from within. Sadly though, a life in the theater was never encouraged. As a matter of fact, in those days it was frowned upon by both our parents as something "nice girls" should never think of doing.

Even today when I go to the theater and watch the actors and dancers and musicians strut their stuff, I revel in their talents and live vicariously though their performances. The child in me is still there deep inside waiting to be a star.

13 WHOSE FOOT IS IT ANYWAY?

"Get your junk off my side of the room," I yelled at my sister, Dorothy. "You are nothing but a slob, and if you don't pick up your mess in the next hour I'm going to toss it all out."

As I stomped out of the room, I heard my sister mumbling something under her breath, which I am sure I was meant to kind of hear.

I went to the living room and slumped down in a big chair. Angrily, I flopped my legs over the arm of the chair, listened to the Lone Ranger on the radio, and watched the minutes tick away on the clock. I was determined she was not going to get a second longer than I had given her. After exactly one hour had passed, I went back into our room and everything was precisely the way it was when I left it. Not a single item had been moved. I told Dorothy, "That's it, I warned you."

At that point I opened the closet door and started tossing every last thing of hers pell-mell into the closet. She ran over to the door and held onto it tightly and dared me to touch anymore of her things. I grabbed the door and slammed it shut....right over her barefoot. She let out a horrible scream....and I fainted dead away on the bedroom floor.

As I was coming to, I heard her saying to my mother, "Why did she faint, it was my foot?"

14 THE ALCATRAZ LIGHTHOUSE

The Alcatraz Lighthouse was not only a beacon to guide ships on the Bay through storms, and fog, and dark of night, it was also home to two Coast Guard families. The Schneider and Davis families each had a daughter. Jacquie Schneider was my age and we spent many wonderful hours in her family's apartment at the top of the Island, doing all those things young girls get involved with during their growing up years.

I remember when Mr. Schneider built a swing outside their living quarters on the cement balcony. Jacquie and I took turns pushing each other up as high as the swing could go to gain height. Our hands gripped the chains that held the swing; we pumped our feet back and forth, and pulled as hard as we could to gain momentum. As we stretched our feet out and pointed them to the sky, it looked as though we had flown over the wall of the balcony and across the Bay. Right between our feet was the skyline of San Francisco and the Golden Gate Bridge. If we had been seagulls, catching the air currents and sailing through the sky, we could not have felt freer.

I laughingly recall that on rainy winter days, after playing inside for hours on end, Jacquie and I would start to get a little stir crazy. Mr. Schneider, sensing our boredom, would say, "Girls, I've got a new stop watch. Why don't you take turns running up the stairs to the light and back down, and I'll time you?" After 120 steps up the narrow circular staircase, and 120 steps down, racing against the clock and each other, we would both collapse on the living room floor, content to rest, giggle, and read the latest edition of Modern Screen Magazine.

I also think back on those wonderful evenings in the fall when the Lighthouse porch took on a totally different feeling. October nights were usually warm, and still, with a million stars glittering in the darkened sky. The boys and girls of all ages, with the blessings of the two Lighthouse families, would gather on the balcony for a dance party. We'd bring a portable wind-up record player called a Victrola, the newest 78s from the Social Hall, and a supply of soft drinks and chips, and talked and danced the evening away. We all learned how to jitterbug, ballroom dance, do the conga, and the Lambeth Walk to the strains of Harry James, Glenn Miller, Kay Kyser's College of Musical Knowledge, and Spike Jones. It was fun for all of us, and also romantic for a few of us. When Mr. Davis and Mr. Schneider came to the door to tell us it was time to end our evening, we would play our final record. Fondly, I remember the warm and new feelings I experienced while dancing close to a special boy, and hearing the words and music of "Goodnight Sweetheart" that signaled the end of a perfect evening.

The Lighthouse Keeper, Edward Schneider, spent 28 years of his life on "The Rock" tending the light and fog signals. But all of us kids remember him most of all for two entirely different reasons. He was the greatest "honky tonk" piano player we had ever heard, and the only musician for a lot of the Island's social functions. Also, because of his rotund 270 pound stature, he played Santa Claus every year at the annual Christmas Party, and never had to "phony it up" by padding himself with pillows.

It never occurred to me that the source of so much enjoyment was directly across from the main entrance to a notorious prison. The guards played an important role in the operation also, because they stood watch 24 hours a day protecting the families who lived there, keeping their lifestyles as normal as possible. All my remembrances of the many hours spent at the Alcatraz Lighthouse remain warm and fuzzy ones. The light and foghorns were not only guardians of the Golden Gate and San Francisco Bay, but a beacon of fun for so many of my young and impressionable years.

Anna Thumann

Mr. Edward Schneider was the Lighthouse keeper on Alcatraz.
(Treasure Island Museum)

15 NAKED ESCAPE

There was a thick, cold, wet fog that completely enveloped the island on a June afternoon in the mid 1930's. As the foghorns bellowed out their haunting wail, the ships on the bay could be heard in a muffled way signaling one another as to their whereabouts. It always frightened me to ride on the bay when the fog was so thick because I imagined that is what it would be like trying to drive a car in total darkness.

Warm and cozy inside the house, dinner was cooking in the oven while my mother and dad were sitting in the living room reading the newspaper and discussing the day's events. My sister and I were sprawled on the floor with books and papers scattered everywhere, trying to get our homework done as soon as possible so we could go to the social hall after dinner and play ping pong. There was always a chance, too, that one of the guards would need a pinsetter in the bowling alley and we could earn some extra money.

The serenity of the setting was suddenly jolted by the terrifying sound of the alarm from the prison - - - very loud blasts that sent a chilling message to all the personnel on the Island that a prison break was in progress. The guards immediately reported to their stations and all the women and children were confined to their living quarters with instructions to lock the doors and windows and not open them to anyone.

Since the house we lived in at that time was in an isolated location by a prison work area, it was more essential than ever we use extraordinary precautions. Our closest neighbors were the Cotterals, and my dad and mother had told us that in the event of a breakout, we were to go immediately to their house, since we would feel safer being with friends. Since none of us had eaten dinner, my mother and Mrs. Cotteral thought a good way to keep the kids occupied was to fix hot dogs, potato chips, and chocolate milk, gather on a blanket on the floor and pretend we were having a picnic.

We talked, and giggled, and talked some more, but as time slowly passed, we could no longer pretend this was just a picnic. The prisoners were still on the loose, the guards were still very much in danger, and a nervous tension permeated the room. Lorraine Cotteral said she would wash the dishes and as she entered the kitchen we heard the dishes crash to the floor and she screamed hysterically, "There's a man outside our house - - - I saw him looking in the window!" She ran into the living room. We huddled together and our mothers put their fingers to their lips and motioned us to be very quiet. Someone started pounding on the kitchen door, and a concerned but familiar voice asked, "Is everyone all right in there?" It was one of the guards and you never saw a more relieved group of people. We unlocked the door and he told us he was sent down to guard our house until the all-clear sounded. Since he had not had any dinner, we handed him a plate of food and locked the door again, and in the darkness we just waited.

We children were getting tired and restless and in order to help us feel more secure, my mom put all three of us together in the big bed upstairs. Needless to say, we never went to sleep and passed the time making up all kinds of spooky horror stories.

Very early in the morning the all-clear sounded and with a collective sigh of relief everyone was reassured the prisoners had been captured in a cave in the rocks down by the water, and none of the island personnel had been harmed in any way. As we all watched, the shackled prisoners were marched from the rocky shore up onto the parade ground. It was then, to the shock of all the onlookers, we saw that the prisoners were stark naked. It was too late to get the women and children back behind closed doors in order to protect the kids from viewing such a spectacle. The inmates were then loaded into the island's only vehicle, "The Black Mariah," and driven up to the prison.

When my dad returned home, my sister and I were "on him" in an instant to ask about the naked men. Most of us girls lived very protected lives and had never seen a naked man, and you can imagine the conversations that took place among us for the next week or so. My dad gave us a very simplified explanation of what happened and it satisfied our curiosity at the time. He said that when prisoners attempted an escape, their focus was to wait for the fog to close in, get down to the edge of the water as fast as possible without being seen, and then collect driftwood from the rocks, take off their clothes and use them to tie the wood together to make a floatation device. They would then rub their bodies with machine oil they had collected from their work areas and get into the bay and try to float undetected to the nearest shore. He explained that the prisoners were so out of condition because of their inactivity during their incarceration, they needed the oil to protect their bodies from the extremely cold temperature of the bay. This time their plans had failed and they never even made it into the bay.

The next day, it was back to school and life as usual. You can guess the questions the Island kids had at school from the teachers and classmates about the escape. But the most fun of all for me was the whispered conversations I had with my closest girlfriends at school giving them the sordid details about what naked grown men really looked like. And believe me, I included all the details that were left out of the physiology books we had looked at in the school library.

All of us had successfully weathered another escape attempt, and the prisoners and island families returned to the task of daily living. The only loss suffered during that turbulent experience was the innocence of some of the young children caught up in the harsh realities of prison life.

These cottages were located on the second level of the Island, half way up the road to the prison and the lighthouse, where they are located at the highest point of the Island.

16 FISH TALES AND ROSES

Just before dawn the guard strolled down the pathway along the sea wall to complete his early morning patrol of the rocky area at the base of the Island. As he directed the light of his flashlight down in the surf he could see the water churning and splashing furiously with huge bass. He ran up the path and yelled to a fellow guard to get the families down there with their fishing gear. Within minutes the rocks were filled with guards, their wives and kids. I was one of those kids, and I remember what fun we all had going wild with enthusiasm over our treasure. The men laid out the fishing tackle, the kids attached the lures to the lines, and as fast as the fish were reeled in the women took the bass off the hooks and put them into tubs of sea water. We pulled in enough bass in a couple of hours to fill the back of the only vehicle on the Island. In that short period of time we caught more fish than was needed for each family to have their fill, and still had plenty to feed the entire prison population.

We experienced a morning that most fishermen only dream about. The fish were running in such large numbers that we only kept the ones weighing twenty pounds or more, and the lighter ones were tossed back into the Bay to be caught another day. My dad told me that the bass were feeding on a school of sardines that was flashing back and forth inside the buoys, and that's what caused such a frenzied commotion. In spite of the fact that the fish were not running in most of the Bay, the fishermen from San Francisco got wind of what was happening on the Island, and tried to edge their boats inside the buoys to get in on the action. The officer in the tower motioned to them repeatedly to get back, and he threatened to fire warning shots over their boats. They were having fits out there watching all the fish that were being caught knowing that they could not legally get any closer to the Island. Needless to say, they were also very frustrated knowing that we didn't even need a license to fish. After all, who was going to get inside the buoys to check us out!

The bass ran in large groups several times a year, following the delicious little sardines or schools of smelt that wiggled and darted around them. But most of the year, fishing was a regular activity for everyone when the weather permitted. As a kid I spent many an hour baiting my hook with the little salted shrimp that I purchased at the Pier 3 Bait Shop in San Francisco. The kids all fished for leopard sharks and sand sharks to give to the prisoner who tended the rose garden at the top of the hill. He was a trustee who was allowed to work in the beautiful rose garden, as well as in the small green house he built for his special plants. We delivered the sharks to the guard, who in turn gave them to the prisoner, and then watched the prisoner dig trenches along the edge of the rose beds and plant the sharks for fertilizer. In return the prisoner would periodically leave a large box of flowers by the fence near the playground, and all of us kids would take a small bouquet to our mothers for the dinner table.

One side effect from all of this was I could never bring myself to eat shrimp. My dad would take me to a nice restaurant in San Francisco and order a shrimp salad. I couldn't believe such a knowledgeable and sophisticated man could sit there and eat fish bait! Of course, now that I am older and wiser. and a devotee of fine food, I love shrimp and know what I am enjoying is not the same stuff that was packed in salt at the Pier 3 Bait Shop.

17 MY FAVORITE TEACHER

Regretfully, she will never know the positive influence she had on my life. Her meticulous grooming, gracious elegance, contagious zest for teaching, made an indelible impression on my young mind. Her manner conveyed not only a gentle side, but also one that commanded respect from everyone who knew her.

Mrs. Fernia D. Acquistapace was my fifth and sixth grade teacher at Sherman Grammar School in San Francisco. At first I was frightened to death of her, while at the same time in awe of her. I had never known anyone quite like her. With no other frame of reference, I thought she was a lady of wealth, status, and knowledge. As a new student to the school and her class, I was convinced right from the start that I would never be able to live up to her high expectations. So, with such a preconceived idea, the first few weeks I just sat quietly and listened and observed. As time went by I grew more comfortable with the daily routines and how she handled various situations. Soon I began to relax and gradually worked up nerve enough to participate in more of the classroom activities.

When it was time to get my first report card, she called my name to pick up the sealed envelope she held in her hand. As I walked to her desk, I was trembling so badly I could hardly make my legs move. Even I knew by now that I was as smart as any of the other kids, I didn't think she knew, because I had been so painfully quiet.

I took the envelope home to my parents, and as I walked in the door my mother asked, "Wasn't today report card day?" I handed her the envelope and waited for her to say something.........anything. I just wanted to put this misery behind me. She opened the card and I saw a smile come to her face. "This is very good, Anna. I'll sign it now and you can take it back to school tomorrow." I took a deep breath and felt the tension flow from my body. The relief was exhilarating, and I had a renewed enthusiasm about going to school.

As I look back on that stage of my life, I realize that our family was affected by the depression, and did not have the means for fancy clothes, or the more visible signs of financial well being. Most students at Sherman School were children of more affluent families living in the Marina District, and even though I was accepted by the kids in my class, I felt like the ugly duckling in my peer group. I was shorter, more protected because of living at the prison, and much less "worldly" than they were. With the subtle encouragement from Mrs. Acquistapace, and the satisfaction from knowing that I was doing well in the classroom, my self image was vastly improved. As our teacher, she had the ability to emotionally connect with each one of us, and make us want to be the best student we could be. We didn't ever want to let her down.

The one experience I fondly remember is that every afternoon while we were doing our silent reading, she would take her hand lotion from her desk drawer, and put a dab on the palm of her hand. As she walked around to the front of her desk to face the class, she would remove her diamond rings from her fingers and slip them on my finger to hold while she massaged the lotion into her hands. I was always seated in the front row in class, and held that job of distinction until I was promoted out of the sixth grade.

Most girls at that time were fans of movie stars, big band singers, and athletes. I liked those celebrities also, but when I grew up I knew I wanted to be just like Mrs. Acquistapace, my favorite teacher of all time. Her actions spoke volumes to me, and I am sorry that as an adult I never took the time to let her know.

18 OUR SPECIAL SECRET

Walter Francis Dorington was my stepfather, but to me he was my dad. As an employee of the federal prison system, he had only one day off from work each week. Often he would take me, all by myself, to the city when my sister and mother didn't want to go. It was always such an exciting time. He and I had a little routine that we went through on those rare occasions. Even though I was too young to actually know what was really going on, I looked forward to it, and treasured every minute.

After the launch docked in the city, we would board the "F" streetcar and ride to Market Street and walk to either the Golden Gate or Warfield Theater. They were the theaters that always had vaudeville along with a movie. My dad would pay for my entrance to the theater, check with the cashier to see how long it would take for the vaudeville show, a movie, the Movietone News, cartoon, Saturday afternoon serial, and the vaudeville show again. Then, at the designated time I would meet him in front of the theater and we would go to Clintons Cafeteria for something to eat. My dad was wonderful to go with to the cafeteria because he would let me slide my tray along the rail and pick out anything I wanted. When I went with my mother, she made all the decisions for me.

After eating our meal, and chattering away about the shows I had seen in the theater, we would make a deal to keep it a secret from mother that he hadn't gone to the movies. After all, we both understood that life would be a lot easier for the whole family if my mother didn't get mad at him.

On our walk to catch the streetcar for our return trip to the dock, my dad would buy me a corsage of either violets or a gardenia, depending on the season of the year. After the vender pinned the flowers on my coat, I felt transformed into Lady Astor. I absolutely loved flowers, and I would care for my corsage as if it were the last flowers I would ever have a chance to feel, and smell, and see.

When we arrived back on the Island my mother would ask my dad about our day, what the movie was about, did we have a good meal, and he would give her all the details. It wasn't until I was much older that I found out that my mother didn't "allow" my dad to drink beer, gamble, and actually gave him an allowance to spend on himself. Also, I realized that on the days off he shared with me, he would go to Chinatown, while I was in the theater, have a beer, and play the Chinese Lottery with HIS share of the movie and lunch money.

My stepfather was the only father I ever knew. He was extremely well educated, kind, smart, even-tempered, and a friend to everyone who knew him, including the prison inmates. He always treated me with respect, and even though he only lived for ten years after he and my mother married, he made an indelible impression on my attitude towards life. Even after I was aware of what was going on during our trips to the city, I was more than happy to go along with his occasional harmless deception. I would even remind him to chew some gum and throw away his lottery ticket stubs before we headed back home.

Walter Dorington (Daddy)

Walter Dorington, Record Clerk/Guard 1934-1943

Daddy, Mother (Margaret) and Dorothy peeking
through on the back porch of our cottage.

19 RIDING THE RAILS

After that wonderful summer of 1940, I felt as though I had grown into a sophisticated, experienced traveler. I was thirteen years old, and was finally given permission to go to downtown San Francisco by myself. Those trips usually involved a boat trip to the city, the "F" streetcar to Powell and Market streets, and then a short walk to the Crystal Palace Market. There I had instructions to buy fresh produce, a few things from the deli and, as written by my mother on the shopping list, some clam chowder for my dad. Of course, it had to be Boston clam chowder and not that red stuff.

But as the summer season was waning, it was time to make arrangements to return to school, and I no longer wanted to be babied. Bravely, I asked my mother (well, to be honest, I really pleaded with my mother) to let me go to an all girls high school. That meant I would have to leave the island earlier in the morning and travel a considerable distance from the dock area to the school at Post and Steiner streets. It would require boarding the "H" streetcar on Van Ness Avenue, and then a transfer at the Lincoln Zephyr Automobile Agency to reach my destination. Much to my surprise, my parents thought that a girls high school sounded like a pretty good idea. On my dad's next day off from work, they took me to the city for a "dry run" on the streetcar so that I would know the exact directions to follow. I was positive I knew the way, but if it made my parents feel good to do this, it was okay with me because from now on I would be on my own.

When the first day of school arrived, I was dressed in my new school clothes, had my new binder on my hip, lunch money wrapped in a hanky in my pocket, and a student pass for the streetcar. After an uneventful boat ride to the city, I hopped off the launch and walked up the hill past the Ghirardelli Chocolate Factory to Van Ness and Bay streets where I boarded the "H" streetcar. I was a little nervous, but I reminded myself that I had traveled to Los Angeles during the summer by myself to visit my grandparents. I got my student pass punched and took a seat beside a window and watched all the familiar landmarks go by. Gradually I realized I didn't recognize anything anymore. Panic set in, and I froze in my seat. The streetcar came to a complete stop and the conductor loudly announced, "End of the line!" What in the world was he talking about....I hadn't reached my transfer street yet. My heart was pounding and I didn't have the foggiest idea where I was or what I was going to do. I sat there, slumped down in my seat, losing all sense of that newfound maturity, and started to cry.

The conductor saw me huddled in my seat and came back to ask if there was a problem. I sobbed my story to him, and that wonderful man told me to take a seat next to him, and on the return trip he would show me where to get off the streetcar. You cannot imagine how stupid and embarrassed I felt when we reached the street where I was supposed to transfer. The conductor told me that toward the end of summer the manufacturer had discontinued making Lincoln Zyphers, and the corner was now the new location for the city's biggest Cadillac agency!

Oh well, so much for the experienced traveler. I did learn one valuable lesson from the misadventure that has served me well through the years. Don't ever tell me a party, a luncheon, or whatever, is at the yellow house in the middle of the block, because with my luck the house has since been painted blue. I only want the name of the street, the house number, and probably a phone number.....just in case I get lost.

By the way, I never told my mother anything about that ride to school.

20 FIRST CRUSH

The first evidence that female hormones were beginning to surface in my very adolescent body was when boys on the Island became much more interesting to me. My good friend, Helen, had two brothers and I thought one of them was really cute. He was smart and good looking, with blue eyes and dark curly hair. The only problem was that he was sixteen years old and I was only twelve. I would hang around and watch him play football, construct beautiful kites out of practically nothing, and build model airplanes in the hallway outside their apartment. I thought he was an absolute genius. He would glue all the colored paper and symbols on the wings of the planes, build boats from tiny little pieces of balsa wood, and assemble racecars that looked exactly like the pictures on the box covers. Whenever I wandered into the hallway on the pretense of looking for his sister, I would stand near his worktable and admire his skills, and revel in the warmth I felt just being near him.

This secret crush was my secret alone. I didn't share my feelings with anyone, not even my best friends. I thought they would all laugh at me, and if he found out about it, he would laugh at me too. I couldn't risk the humiliation and blow to my ego. The only time that I was really able to express my feelings was on Valentines Day, and each year I searched the dime stores in San Francisco to find just the right card to be delivered at just the right moment.

It was part of the Valentine ritual to buy cards for everyone in my class at school, and for all the kids my age on the Island. After signing and addressing the cards, I would slip that special Valentine I had found for my secret crush in the pocket of my bathrobe, and made an excuse to lock myself in the bathroom. There I would read the card over and over, imagining the thrill and curiosity he would feel from such a loving message.

Roses are red, Violets are blue, I like you a lot. Hope you like me too.

Then I would carefully print his name on the envelope and sign the card "ME."

On the night of February 14th it was usually cold, stormy, and very wet on the Island. I would gather the cards in a bag, and then dressed in my yellow rain slicker and goulashes I walked to each house or apartment. I would quietly slip a card under the door, knock a couple of times and then run and hide. I put the cards for my secret crush's brother and sister under their door first and then after I finished delivering valentines to all my friends on the Island, I would go back to my secret crush's apartment put his card under the door. That way I was sure they would not guess it came from the same person who had been there earlier.

Back home from my adventure, I would excitedly pick up all the cards that had been delivered to my house while I was gone, eagerly anticipating that special Valentine I prayed I would get from my secret love. My heart would sink when it wasn't there, but I had a warm feeling knowing that he would read my card and be intrigued by who had sent it.

I continued to admire him from afar for several years. When WWII was declared, and the eligible young men from the Island volunteered for service, I was only fourteen and devastated at the pending loss of my secret love. One evening a few weeks before he left for Boot Camp, I bravely told him how I felt, and how embarrassed I was knowing that in his eyes I was much too young for him to think of me as his girlfriend. To my amazement, he confessed that he had felt the same way about me for years, but had kept it to himself for exactly the same reasons. That night, right there in the darkened hallway near his worktable, he put his arms around me and gave me my very first "real" kiss, and I knew I was in love. A week or so later when he was preparing to leave, he gave me a goodbye kiss and handed me a locket with his picture in it for me to wear near my heart.

But, life goes on, and after the passage of time and a few letters from the South Pacific, we lost touch with one another. Like so many "first crushes," the experience will always remain as a fond memory from my past.

21 THE DAY MY WORLD CHANGED

We wanted so badly to beat those guys on Angel Island, we could taste it! They had so many more kids to choose from, but we thought with lots of practice, and an infallible game plan, we could win the battle of the Islands.

This football game had been in the works for a long time. Each year the kids from Angel Island would challenge the kids from Alcatraz to a flag football game. Most of us rode the General Frank M. Coxe, nicknamed "The Coxie" by the kids, to or from school during the week. Consequently, we had great discussions about all the various games we played during the year. But the football season always brought out the braggadocios nature of all the kids, especially the older boys. Angel Island was an Army post and housed a great many families with a large population of children. Our Island was only twelve acres, most of which were taken up by the prison grounds, and we had a small, but very select, population of kids.

Since our Island's grounds were nearly all cement, we practiced on a pretty tough field. There was a surface in front of Building #64 where we could measure the length and width to approximate the real football field we would be using on Angel Island. Our "field" was long enough, but the width left a lot to be desired. We had to jump a few curbs as we were running, but we got used to it and it was no longer a problem. We had a few skinned knees and elbows, but we were used to that since cement was all we ever had to play on. This time the teams had to be made up of "boys only," so we had to use boys of all ages to get an eleven man team, and still have a few substitutes. Herbie, Dick, Bob, and Hank were all in high school, so they made sure they got the "glory spots" on the team. Their younger brothers were designated to do whatever the older boys told them to do. Since they needed a team to practice against, the girls were coerced into being "Angel Island." One of the mothers sewed all the time, and she had lots of extra material and made the flags for the team's back pockets. She also helped us girls to make pom-poms out of the same color so that we could go along and show Angel Island our cheerleading skills.

The day finally arrived and we all remembered to pack lunches, football equipment, pom poms and flags, and meet on the dock no later than 10:50 a.m. on Sunday morning, December 7, 1941. "The Coxie" was on its way from Fort Mason, and was scheduled to pick us up at exactly 11:00 a.m. for the twenty-minute ride to Angel Island. The game was going to begin at 12:00 noon and parents who were interested were also invited to attend. It was going to be such a fun day. Each team had won a game before, so this game would determine the championship. I should interject that Angel Island was always better than we were, but the last time we played, they had an epidemic of chickenpox, which wrecked their team and, to our delight, we won in a big way.

A few minutes before "The Coxie" arrived, we saw the guards who had just checked us all "off the Island" for the day, scurrying around in a very frantic and chaotic way, and we all instinctively knew that something horrible was wrong. "The Coxie" docked, but no one lowered the gangplank for us to board. Mr. Simpson gathered us together and brought us into the office on the dock and told us that Japan had bombed Pearl Harbor and that Angel Island, which housed Fort McDowell, was closed to everyone as they had received orders to prepare their troops for war in the South Pacific.

We were stunned --- we didn't know how to react, or respond, or really what to do. All of a sudden our excitement over the much anticipated game had evaporated, and we just waited for someone, anyone, to tell us what to do. Our parents came down to the dock and took us back to our homes. I remember hearing Herbie, Dick, Bob and Hank all talking excitedly about signing up for the service. I had seen the newsreels about the war at the movies, and listened to President Roosevelt talk about the news from Europe on the radio, but it all seemed so far away from my little world in the middle of the Bay. It had never entered my mind that my childhood friends would soon be going off, to heaven only knows where, to risk their lives for those of us at home. In my own isolated, cozy, wonderful, secure world that I imagined would go on forever, the rug had been pulled out from under my feet. For the first time, I felt scared of the future, unsure of myself and my role in all of this, and so frightened for the boys, who just a few short minutes ago were destined to be our heroes – and champions of the Islands.

The older group of "Kids" that lived on the Island in early 1941.

22 MY SPECIAL WORLD

The seawall, on the Island where I lived, was sometimes a refuge, sometimes a secret hiding place, and sometimes a place to play with my friends. As I remember it, the wall was about three feet high, and extended from the Golden Gate side of the parade ground all the way around to the beginning of the steps by Building #64. It had been built with rocks from the Island, and eventually became overgrown by a thick layer of beautiful Persian Carpet. The rocky area leading up to the wall from the Bay was covered with a mass of the Persian Carpet intermingled with ice plant. At various times of the year the lavender flowers on the carpet, and the varied colors of the flowering ice plant, were spectacular

My first excursion to the seawall was during the summer of '34. As I stood there I could see San Francisco, the tip of Marin County, Goat Island, Angel Island, the campanile at U.C. Berkeley, and ferry boats traversing back and forth across the bay. On other occasions I watched the large ocean liners, with musicians playing on deck and revelers noisily celebrating, as they headed out through the Gate to some exotic location in the South Pacific. I wondered what they were doing, where they were going, and what it must be like to be rich and free to go anywhere in the world without any worries. At such a young age, my only frame of reference was what I saw in the movies, and I could only vicariously live those marvelous experiences through my imagination.

During the next ten years or so, from my perch on the wall, I watched the Golden Gate Bridge being built. I also saw all the pieces put into place for the Bay Bridge, and I watched the gigantic cranes and barges dump dirt into the Bay, as they created a brand new island, which was eventually called Treasure Island. I watched the first airborne clippers fly from across the Bay and over the Golden Gate Bridge, with their final destination either Hawaii or China.

During the years before WWII, I sat on the wall and gazed for hours as the Pacific fleet sailed in through the Gate and anchored in the Bay. I learned to recognize a submarine, a cruiser, a destroyer, a tender, and a battle ship, and after a few years I could even spot them by name as they came into view. But, sadly, with the advent of December 7, 1941, the Navy learned a very difficult lesson and never gathered its ships en masse again.

My seawall was my place of solace, and an ever-changing panoramic view of my little world. But now, after all these years, I can still close my eyes and savor the crisp sea breeze against my cheeks, smell the freshness of the sea, and feel incredibly nostalgic about the history I was privileged to observe. As a young girl those years were just fun for me, but the older I get, the more poignant the memories become, and the more truly blessed I know I am to have experienced such a unique childhood.

UNITED STATES OF AMERICA
OFFICE OF PRICE ADMINISTRATION
WAR RATION BOOK TWO
IDENTIFICATION

Tolksdorf, Anna Elizabeth
(Name of person to whom book is issued)

(Street number or rural route)

Alcatraz Island   California   15
(City or post office)   (State)   (Age)   (Sex)

ISSUED BY LOCAL BOARD No. 11 - 2   S. F.
(County)

OFFICE OF PRICE ADM.
49375

Cal
(State)

2150 Union St.
(Street address of local board)

S. F.
(City)

By Mrs. E. T. Allen
(Signature of issuing officer)

SIGNATURE Anna Elizabeth Tolksdorf
(To be signed by the person to whom this book is issued. If such person is unable to sign because of age or incapacity, another may sign in his behalf)

WARNING

1 This book is the property of the United States Government. It is unlawful to sell or give it to any other person or to use it or permit anyone else to use it, except to obtain rationed goods for the person to whom it was issued.
2 This book must be returned to the War Price and Rationing Board which issued it, if the person to whom it was issued is inducted into the armed services of the United States, or leaves the country for more than 30 days, or dies. The address of the Board appears above.
3 A person who finds a lost War Ration Book must return it to the War Price and Rationing Board which issued it.
4 PERSONS WHO VIOLATE RATIONING REGULATIONS ARE SUBJECT TO $10,000 FINE OR IMPRISONMENT, OR BOTH.

OPA Form No. R-131   16—30565-1

During the Second World War, certain items were in short supply and were subject to rationing by the government. Among the items rationed at sometime during the war were tires, cars, gasoline, sugar, coffee, meat, cheese, shoes and even typewriters.

UNITED STATES OF AMERICA

War Ration Book One

WARNING

1 Punishments ranging as high as *Ten Years' Imprisonment or $10,000 Fine, or Both,* may be imposed under United States Statutes for violations thereof arising out of infractions of Rationing Orders and Regulations.

2 This book must not be transferred. It must be held and used only by or on behalf of the person to whom it has been issued, and anyone presenting it thereby represents to the Office of Price Administration, an agency of the United States Government, that it is being so held and so used. For any misuse of this book it may be taken from the holder by the Office of Price Administration.

3 In the event either of the departure from the United States of the person to whom this book is issued, or his or her death, the book must be surrendered in accordance with the Regulations.

4 Any person finding a lost book must deliver it promptly to the nearest Ration Board.

Nº 120188 -45

OFFICE OF PRICE ADMINISTRATION

The Stamps contained in this Book are valid only after the lawful holder of this Book has signed the certificate below, and are void if detached contrary to the Regulations. (A father, mother, or guardian may sign the name of a person under 18.) In case of questions, difficulties, or complaints, consult your local Ration Board.

Certificate of Book Holder

I, *the undersigned,* do hereby certify that I have observed all the conditions and regulations governing the issuance of this War Ration Book; that the "Description of Book Holder" contained herein is correct; that an application for issuance of this book has been duly made by me or on my behalf; and that the statements contained in said application are true to the best of my knowledge and belief.

Anna Elizabeth Tolksdorf   [Book Holder's Own Name]

(Signature of, or on behalf of, Book Holder)

Any person signing on behalf of Book Holder must sign his or her own name below

and indicate relationship to Book Holder

Margaret Dorington   *Mother*

(Father, Mother, or Guardian)

★ U. S. GOVERNMENT PRINTING OFFICE : 1942   16—26651-1

OPA Form No. R-302

23 EPILOGUE

I still live in the Bay Area in Northern California. My two sons have grown to be fine young men, and are currently living their own lives and building their own memoirs. Many of my stories about my experiences on Alcatraz Island have appeared in various publications.

I was born in Maryland in 1927, and at the age of 84 I still enjoy writing and trying to learn something new each day.

**Alcatraz Island Family
75th Anniversary
2009**

ALCATRAZ
IS SPANISH
FOR PELICAN

ALCATRAZ ISLAND, CALIF.

Anna Thumann

There currently are two Alcatraz Alumni organizations. The Alcatraz Island Family is the original group made up of members who were part of the early families that moved to the Island. The Alcatraz Alumni Association is more a business organization, with many members who lived on the Island and many who are just interested in being involved with events on the Island.

MEMBER *thru July* 2011

Department of Justice
United States Penitentiary, Alcatraz Island, California

IDENTIFICATION CARD

This is to certify that

Anna Tolksdorf

whose signature appears on the margin hereof is a relative of -

Mr. W. F. Dorington (Record Clerk)

This card is to be used as a pass only by the person to whom issued in accordance with regulations governing.

Signature:

11/14/40
(Date of issue)   WARDEN

An Identification Card was issued to all Alcatraz Island personnel. It was used to identify each person upon leaving and arriving on the Island to verify their residency. It was also used to take a short cut through Fort Mason when walking to school.

The person to whom this pass is issued is cautioned not to allow it to be used by any other person.

It is intended to aid identification and to facilitate arrival and departure with the minimum of restriction consistent with maximum safety.

The authorized holder must be prepared to present it on arriving and departing and whenever requested by guard.

Upon termination of service of the related officer, removal from the Island, or breach of regulations, the card must be returned to the Warden.

U.S.P.A.C.F, 28

ABOUT THE AUTHOR

This is Anna Thumann's first published book. She has had stories about her ten years on Alcatraz Island published in the San Jose Mercury News, and WritersTalk, the monthly newsletter of the South Bay Writers Club. She, her two sons, and their families all reside in Northern California.

Made in the USA
Charleston, SC
30 June 2011